PURDY'S INSTRUMENT HANDBOOK
by Ralph Dewey

© Copyright 2015 by Ralph Dewey
Revised and Expanded

Glen Enterprises
PO Box 1201
Deer Park, TX 77536-1201

D1211858

OUR PURPOSE

This book represents years of instrument experience and know-how. It contains notes, examples, procedures, hook-up drawings and tables. Since most of the information is general in nature, there will be exceptions and cases where it will not be applicable. Information in this book is not intended to overrule common sense or to violate any safety procedures or laws. Before using any of this information, check with an instrument engineer to determine if it is appropriate for your application. It is assumed that the reader/user has some basic instrumentation knowledge and experience. Instrument craftsmen, operators and engineers will find it useful as a quick reference. It is a field book, rather than a textbook. We have tried to make all of the information useful, clear and accurate. However, neither the author or publisher shall be held responsible for any errors in content or the application of the information in this book or any damages or loses from its use. If you have any suggestions for this book, write and let us know about them.

ISBN 1-880215-26-8

ABBREVIATIONS, ACRONYMS & TERMS

I.A.S	Instrument Air Supply
FC	Fail Closed
FO	Fail Open
FL	Fail Locked (Fail in Place)
A/O	Air to Open
A/C	Air to Close
ATC	Air to Close
ATO	Air to Open
S.P.	Set Point
I/P	Current to Pneumatic Transducer
I/O	Input/Output
SCFM	Standard Cubic Feet per Minute
SCFH	Standard Cubic Feet per Hour
GPM	Gallons Per Minute
GPH	Gallons Per Hour
UPS	Uninterruptible Power Supply
dBA	Decibels (or dB)
pH	Acid/Caustic term
DVOM	Digital Volt, Ohm, Meter
P.S.	Power Supply
DCS	Distributed Control System

MORE TERMS

VDC	Volts Direct Current
VAC	Volts Alternating Current
LRV	Lower Range Value
URV	Upper Range Value
M/R	Minutes per Repeat
R/M	Repeats per Minute
Dir.	Direct
Rev.	Reverse
Inc./Inc.	Increase/Increase (direct)
Inc./Dec.	Increase/Decrease (reverse)
D/P	Differential Pressure

DEFINITIONS

Alignment Adjusting the various parts of a controller to make them work together properly, thus eliminating offset.

Analog Signal A signal that has an infinite number of values and varies in strength rather than digital pulses. Two common types are 4-20 milliamps and 3-15 psig.

Automatic Controller A device that compares process conditions with the set point and generates the appropriate corrective action.

4

Calibration The adjustment of a measuring device (transmitter, gauge, transducer, etc.) for the best accuracy of its range, signal or set value.

Closed Loop A control system where process changes are continually measured and compared to a set point so corrective actions can be implemented automatically.

Cascade Control Automatic control involving the cascading of controllers such that the output of one controller varies the set point of another controller.

Controller Feedback The input signal to the controller representing the condition of the controlled variable either positive or negative.

Derivative Action A control mode that provides a temporary output boost based upon the RATE of the process change. The faster the process changes, the greater the derivative action.

Digital Signal A signal that has only two values, on and off. One type of digital signal uses a series of on/off pulses to communicate information.

Elevation In level applications, compensation for an unwanted signal on the low pressure side of a differential level transmitter.

Range the lowest and highest values where a device or instrument operates. A range is always expressed with two numbers, the lower range values (LRV) and the upper value (URV).

Ratio Controller A controller that maintains a fixed ratio between two or more process flows.

Set Point   The desired process value that a controller or control system is asked to maintain.

Span The numeric difference between the lower and upper range values. It is always expressed as a single numeric value.

Suppression In level applications, compensation for an unwanted signal on the high pressure side of a differential level transmitter.

Transducer An instrument device that translates one type or form of a signal into another type. An I/P transducer converts a 4-20 ma input signal into a 3-15 psig output signal.

Viscosity A term representing the resistance of a fluid to flow.

+++

Maintenance Tip
Ensure that 3-valve instrument manifolds are not installed backwards on flow loops. Do not use 3-valve manifolds on level loops that have seal legs. There is a risk of losing the seal fluid if the by-pass valve is accidentally opened.

COMMON INSTRUMENT SYMBOLS

PRESSURE TRANSMITTER

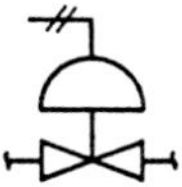

CONTROL VALVE

INSTRUMENT SUPPLY OR PROCESS CONNECTION

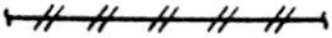

PNEUMATIC SIGNAL LINE

ELECTRICAL SIGNAL

CAPILLARY TUBING

HYDRAULIC LINE

ELECTROMAGNETIC OR SONIC SIGNAL (GUIDED)

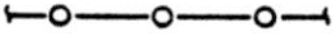

SOFTWARE OR DATA LINK

7

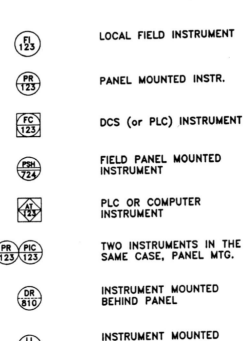

LOCAL FIELD INSTRUMENT

PANEL MOUNTED INSTR.

DCS (or PLC) INSTRUMENT

FIELD PANEL MOUNTED
INSTRUMENT

PLC OR COMPUTER
INSTRUMENT

TWO INSTRUMENTS IN THE
SAME CASE, PANEL MTG.

INSTRUMENT MOUNTED
BEHIND PANEL

INSTRUMENT MOUNTED
BEHIND FIELD PANEL

8

Common Instrument Prefixes For Loops

AT	Analyzer Transmitter
AIC	Analyzer Indicating Controller
CT	Conductivity Transmitter
DT	Density (or Specific Gravity) Transmitter
EIT	Voltage (EMF) Indicating Transmitter
FIC	Flow Indicating Controller
FO	Flow Orifice (Restriction Orifice)
FE	Flow Element (flow measuring device)
FQR	Flow Integrator (Totalizer) Recorder
FFC	Flow Fraction (Ratio) Controller
HS	Hand Switch
IR	Current Recorder
JR	Power Recorder
LG	Level Glass
LSH	Level Switch High
LAHH	Level Alarm High High (Could be a shutdown)
PIC	Pressure Indicating Controller
PDI	Pressure Differential indicator
PV	Pressure Valve (Control Valve)
PCV	Pressure Control Valve (Regulator)

PDT	Pressure Differential Transmitter
PSL	Pressure Switch Low
PSLL	Pressure Switch Low Low
PY	Pressure Relay or Computing Device (Could be an I/P Transducer)
RIC	Radiation Indicating Controller
ST	Speed Transmitter
TT	Temperature Transmitter
TE	Temperature Element
TJ	Temperature Scan
TV	Temperature Valve
TCV	Temperature Control Valve (Process-powered Temp. Regulator)
TW	Temperature Well (Thermowell)
WE	Weight (or force) Element
ZL	Position Light (pilot)
ZSC	Position Switch Closed
ZSO	Position Switch Open
UT	Multivariable Transmitter
VT	Vibration Transmitter
WT	Weight/Force Transmitter
YI	Event/State/Pressure Indicator

Specific Gravity and Liquid Viscosities

Approximate values at standard conditions. (Temp. changes will vary values.)

	S.G.	centipoises
Acetic acid	1.050	1.40
Acetone	.792	.350
Benzene	.879	.655
Butene	.6013	.154
Ethylene glycol	1.125	25
Gasoline	.751	.69
Hexane	.664	.30
Hydrochloric Acid	1.64	3.1
Isobutane	.5361	.175
Kerosene	.820	2.2
Nitric Acid -100%	1.50	2.8
Phosphoric Acid	1.87	.12
Silicone (DC-200)	.920	350
Sodium Hydroxide - 30%	1.33	13.0
Sulfuric Acid	1.83	26.7
Water	1.00	1.12

Standard Conditions are 14.7 PSIA and 60°F. However some rotameter companies use other values.

PRESSURE CONVERSION FACTORS

⊗ Example: 25 PSI times 6.895 equals 172.375 kPa (Kilopascals)

	PSI	ATM.	LB/FT2	IN. H2O	FT. H2O	MM Hg.	IN. Hg.	kPa	Kg/CM2
PSI	1	.068	144.0	27.73	2.3108	51.715	2.036	6.895	.0703
ATM.	14.69	1	2116	407.51	33.959	760.0	29.921	101.32	1.0332
LB/FT2	.0069	.00047	1	.193	.016	.3604	.0142	.04789	.00048
IN. H2O	.0361	.00245	5.19	1	.08333	1.865	.07342	.24864	.00253
FT. H2O	.4327	.02945	62.4	12	1	22.38	.88108	2.9836	.03042
MM Hg.	.0193	.00131	2.77	.5362	.04468	1	.03937	.13332	.00136
IN. Hg.	.4911	.03342	70.47	13.619	1.1349	25.4	1	3.3864	.03453
kPa	.1450	.00987	20.88	4.0218	.3352	7.5006	.2953	1	.01019
Kg/CM2	14.22	.96784	2048.2	394.41	32.868	735.56	28.959	98.066	1

IN. H2O is inches of water, FT. H2O is feet of water, ATM. is atmosphere
Kg/CM2 is Kilograms per Centimeter Squared, LB/FT2 is pounds per square foot
MM Hg. is millimeters of Mercury, IN. Hg. is inches of Mercury
IN. H2O and FT. H2O are at 20 °C, MM H2O and IN. Hg. are at 0 °C
IN. H2O at 15.5 °C (60 °F) times .578 = Ounces (oz.) of H2O
Ounces (oz.) of H2O times 1.730092 = IN. H2O at 15.5 °C (60 °F)

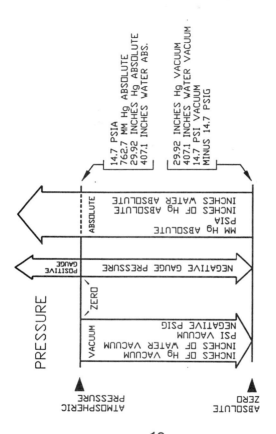

PRESSURE

14.7 PSIA ABSOLUTE
762.7 MM Hg ABSOLUTE
29.92 INCHES Hg ABSOLUTE
407.1 INCHES WATER ABS.

29.92 INCHES Hg VACUUM
407.1 INCHES WATER VACUUM
14.7 PSI VACUUM
MINUS 14.7 PSIG

ABSOLUTE

INCHES WATER ABSOLUTE
INCHES OF Hg ABSOLUTE
PSIA
MM Hg ABSOLUTE

POSITIVE GAUGE

NEGATIVE GAUGE PRESSURE

ZERO

VACUUM

INCHES OF Hg VACUUM
INCHES OF WATER VACUUM
PSI VACUUM
NEGATIVE PSIG

ATMOSPHERIC PRESSURE

ABSOLUTE ZERO

13

Special Pressure Conversions

The following formulas are for special pressures or for pressure terms that go in opposite directions

407.1 - MM Hg X .534) = Inches Water Vacuum
Example: 407.1 minus 120 millimeters of mercury
         times .534 = 343.02 inches of water vacuum

407.1 - In. HG abs. X 13.6 = Inches Water Vacuum
29.92 - In. Water abs. X .0735 = Inches Hg Vacuum
762.7 - In. Water Vac. X 1.87 = MM Hg Absolute
407.1 - PSIA X 27.7 = Inches of Water Vacuum
14.7 - PSIA = PSI Vacuum
14.7 - Negative PSIG = PSIA
14.7 - In. Water Vac. X .0361) = PSIA
407.1 - Inches Water abs. = Inches Water Vacuum
407.1 - Inches Water vac. = Inches Water Absolute
 * Normally MM Hg is understood to be Absolute
+++
   1 gallon of water = 8.33 pounds
   Density of water = 62.5 lb./cubic foot
   1 cubic foot of water = 7.481 gallons
   1 gallon = .13368 cubic foot
   1 gallon = 231 cubic inches
   1 cubic foot = 1,728 cubic inches
   Centipoise = (Centistokes)(Specific Gravity)

CONVERSION FACTORS

Mw = Molecular Weight
PPH = Pounds Per Hour
SCFH = Standard Cubic Feet Per Hour
SCFM = Standard Cubic Feet Per Minute
S.G. = Specific Gravity
GPM = Gallons Per Minute

GAS FLOW FORMULAS

$$SCFH = \frac{PPH}{Mw} (379.2)$$

$$SCFH = \frac{PPH}{LB/FT^3 @ BASE}$$

$$SCFM = \frac{13.1}{S.G.} (PPM)$$

$$SCFM = \frac{(PPH)(6.3)}{Mw}$$

$$PPH = (SCFH)(S.G.)(.0764)$$

$$PPH = \frac{(Mw)(SCFH)}{379.2}$$

$$PPH = \frac{(Mw)(SCFM)}{6.32}$$

LIQUID FLOW

$$GPM = \frac{PPH}{(8.3378)(*S.G.)(60)}$$

$$PPH = (8.3378)(*S.G.)(GPM)(60)$$

* S.G. at flowing conditions

$$GPM = (449)(CFS)$$

CFS = Cubic Feet Per Second

FLOW [Metric to USA]

cm3/min	X	.00026417	= GPM
cm3/min	X	.002118	= SCFH
L/min	X	.26417	= GPM
L/min	X	2.118	= SCFH
m3/min	X	264.17	= GPM
m3/min	X	2118.88	= SCFH

FLOW [USA to Metric]

GPM	X	3788	= cm3/min
GPM	X	3.788	= L/min
GPM	X	.003788	= m3/min
SCFH	X	472.14	= cm3/min
SCFH	X	.472	= L/min
SCFH	X	.000472	= m3/min

DENSITY FORMULA

PSIA = Pounds Per Square Inch Absolute
Zf = Compressibility Factor
lb/ft3 = Pounds Per Cubic Foot

$$lb/ft3 = \frac{(Mw)(PSIA)}{(10.73)(460 + deg. F)(Zf)}$$

Metric Unit Prefixes

Prefix	Symbol	Power of 10		Numerical Value
mega	M	10^6	million	1,000,000
kilo	k	10^3	thousand	1,000
		10^0	one	1
deci	d	10^{-1}	tenth	.1
centi	c	10^{-2}	hundredth	.01
milli	m	10^{-3}	thousandth	.001
micro	μ	10^{-6}	millionth	.000 001
pico	p	10^{-12}	trillionth	.000 000 000 001

SAFETY TIP

Before removing a transmitter, check to see if it is part of a shutdown system, double check that you are on the correct instrument, and make sure the control loop is in manual.

METRIC DECIMAL CONVERSION   < = MOVE DECIMAL TO LEFT,   > = TO THE RIGHT

	Mega	Kilo	Basic Unit	Deci	Centi	Milli	Micro	Pico
Mega		3 >	6 >	7 >	8 >	9 >	12 >	18 >
Kilo	< 3		3 >	4 >	5 >	6 >	9 >	15 >
Basic Unit	< 6	< 3		1 >	2 >	3 >	6 >	12 >
Deci	< 7	< 4	< 1		1 >	2 >	5 >	11 >
Centi	< 8	< 5	< 2	< 1		1 >	4 >	10 >
Milli	< 9	< 6	< 3	< 2	< 1		3 >	9 >
Micro	< 12	< 9	< 6	< 5	< 4	< 3		6 >
Pico	< 18	< 15	< 12	< 11	< 10	< 9	< 6	

EXAMPLE: TO GO FROM CENTI TO MICRO MOVE DECIMAL POINT 4 PLACES RIGHT

SAFETY TIP

When bleeding off a transmitter, have you checked the direction of the wind? Do you have an escape path? Could the product drip on workers below? Should it be routed to a vent header?

LOOP LOAD LIMITATIONS

The typical "Two-Wire" transmitter loop uses a 24 VDC power supply voltage and has a total resistance of about 255 to 260 ohms. That would be the DCS input resistor (250 ohms) plus a small amount of lead wire resistance. There is a limit to how many devices that can be added to a "Two-Wire" loop. If your supply is 24 VDC, the maximum load is 600 ohms. Use the formula below for other supply voltages.

$$\text{Power Supply Voltage} = \frac{\text{Max. Load}}{50} + 12$$

If your total resistance is 800 ohms, for example, you will need at least 28 VDC. Most DCS systems are designed with a fixed 24 VDC supply so if an increase is needed, a field power supply will be needed.

NEC® is a registered trademark of the National Fire Protection Association, Inc., Quincy, MA.

Understanding 4-20 ma Signals

Transmitter Two-wire transmitters are often powered by 24VDC and have a circuit which maintains its 4-20ma output current to correlate to the process input value applied to the transmitter's sensor. You will measure about 24VDC across the transmitter wires in the field. Controller outputs are different.

Controller The output signal in a 4-20 ma controller uses a dependent current circuit. Even with various loop resistance values, it will maintain the DC ma output that the controller desires as its output. The controller's output voltage adjusts as needed so that it maintains the desired loop current signal to an I/P or other device. Therefore you will often measure controller output voltages less than 4 VDC.

++++++++++++++++++++++++++++++++++

Maintenance Tip

Loops that are powered from the field will be terminated on the DCS differently than loops which get their 24VDC power from the DCS.

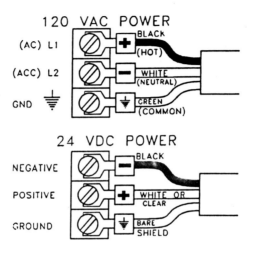

SAFETY TIP
Always use one hand to measure voltages. Keep the other hand in your pocket to prevent a path through your heart.

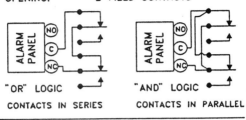

FAILSAFE ALARM (HAS CONTINUITY)
CLOSED LOOP, ALARMS UPON FIELD DEVICE
OPENING.   2 FIELD CONTACTS

"OR" LOGIC

CONTACTS IN SERIES

"AND" LOGIC

CONTACTS IN PARALLEL

NON–FAILSAFE ALARM (NO CONTINUITY)
OPEN LOOP, ALARMS UPON FIELD DEVICE
CLOSURE.   2 FIELD CONTACTS

"OR" LOGIC

CONTACTS IN PARALLEL

"AND" LOGIC

CONTACTS IN SERIES

SAFETY TIP
**If you discover an electrical shock victim that is
still touching wires, use a non-conductor to pull
the victim clear or to pull off the wires.**

SPECIAL PRESSURE GAUGE SITUATIONS

Some products like liquid hydrogen peroxide and metal alkyls shouldn't be blocked in. If a gauge inadvertently gets blocked in, without venting off the process, they can soon pressure up and blow apart the gauge. The 3-way valve arrangements below safely blocks in the process and vents off the product. The left drawing is of an open valve. The right drawing is of a blocked valve that vents off the process at the same time.

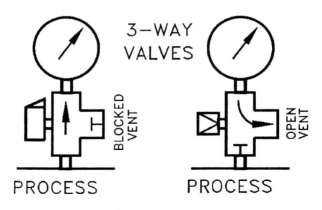

FAILSAFE LEVEL SWITCH HIGH

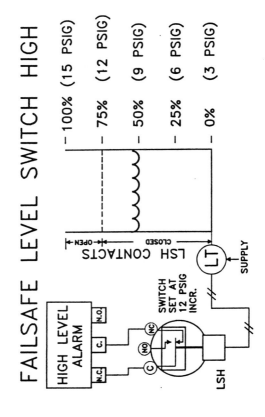

One way to dampen wild, noisy, oscillating or fluctuating pneumatic signals is to use an inverse derivative device like the Moore Products model 59R. Dial in the amount of dampening to make the signal stable.

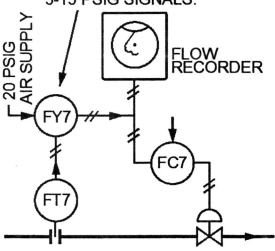

MOORE PRODUCTS 59R SIGNAL
DAMPENER FOR NOISY
3-15 PSIG SIGNALS.

FLOW
RECORDER

20 PSIG
AIR SUPPLY

FY7

FC7

FT7

SIMPLE FAILSAFE ALARM WITH ACKNOWLEDGE PLUS TEST LIGHT AND HORN.

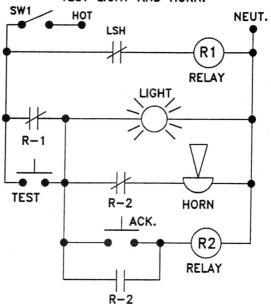

THERMOCOUPLE INFORMATION

TYPE	+ WIRE	- WIRE	MAX.RANGE
J	Iron White (magnetic)	Constantan Red	0 to 1200 F
E	Chromel Purple	Constantan Red	-300 to 1600 F
K	Chromel Yellow	Alumel Red (magnetic)	800 to 2000 F
T	Copper Blue	Constantan Red	-300 to 200 F

THERMOCOUPLE ARRANGEMENTS

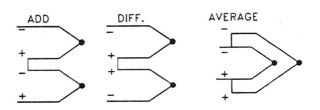

TEMPERATURE CONVERSION CHART

FROM \ TO	°C CELSIUS	°F FARENHEIT	K KELVIN	°R RANKINE	°r RÉAUMUR
°C	1.0	1.8(°C)+32	°C+273.15	1.8(°C)+491.67	(.8)°C
°F	(°F-32)5/9	1.0	5/9(°F)+255.37	°F+459.67	(°F-32)4/9
K	K-273.15	(K)1.8-459.67	1.0	(K)1.8	(K-273.15)*(4/5)
°R	(°R-491.67)*(5/9)	°R-459.67	5/9(°R)	1.0	(°R-491.67)*(4/5)
°r	5/4(°r)	9/4(°r)+32	5/4(°r)+273.15	9/4(°r)+491.67	1.0

Note: Kelvin does not use the degree symbol.

EXAMPLE: 50 °F-32(5/9)=10 °C

°F=1.8(°C)+32   °C=(°F-32).5555

K=°C+273.15   °R=459.69+°F

29

100 OHM RTD CHART

Resistance vs Temperature for a 100 ohm platinum RTD (Alpha = .00385) DIN 43760 and BS 1904

Degree F	Degree C	Ohms
1000	537.78	293.49
900	482.22	275.04
800	426.67	256.23
700	371.11	237.07
600	315.56	217.55
500	260.00	197.69
400	204.44	177.47
300	148.89	156.90
200	93.33	135.97
150	65.56	125.37
100	37.78	114.68
50	10.00	103.90
----	----	----
32	0.0	100.00
----	----	----
0	-17.78	93.03
-50	-45.56	82.06
-100	-73.33	70.98

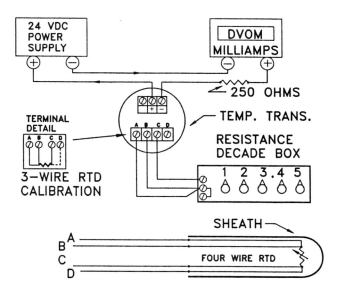

SAFETY TIP

Don't try to remove pistons from piston actuators by applying air pressure. The piston could shoot out like a cannon ball and injure someone.

LINEAR INTERPOLATION

Find the ohmic value for 420 degrees F. When only given values above and below it.

$450° = 187.62\Omega, \quad 400° = 177.47\Omega$

$$\frac{450 - 400}{187.62 - 177.47} = \frac{420 - 400}{X - 177.47}$$

$$\frac{50}{10.15} = \frac{20}{X - 177.47}$$

$$50 (X - 177.47) = 203$$

$X = 181.53$ Ohms $[420°F = 181.53\Omega]$

MAINTENANCE TIP

Make sure that all RTD and thermocouple sensors are fully "bottomed out" in their thermowells. All temperature sensors must make firm contact in order to sense the process temperature correctly.

Instrument Signal Conversion Formulas

* Use percentage fractions for calculating.

Percentage	0%	25%	50%	75%	100%
4-20 mA	4	8	12	16	20
1-5 VDC	1	2	3	4	5
3-15 psig	3	6	9	12	15

mA - 4 $\div$ 16 $\times$ 100 = % $\bullet$ % $\div$ 100 $\times$ 16 + 4 = mA

VDC -1 $\div$ 4 $\times$ 100 = % $\bullet$ % $\div$ 100 $\times$ 4 + 1 = VDC

PSIG -3 $\div$ 12 $\times$ 100 = % $\bullet$ % $\div$ 100 $\times$ 12 + 3 = PSIG

Example: 15 mA equates to what signal %?
 15 mA - 4 $\div$ 16 $\times$ 100 = .6875 or 68.75%
Example: A 40% signal equates to what mA?
 .40 $\div$ 100 $\times$ 16 + 4 = 10.4 mA

Convert 4-20 mA to 1-5 VDC
mA - 4 $\div$ 16 $\times$ 4 + 1 = VDC

Convert 4-20 mA to 3-15 psig
mA - 4 $\div$ 16 $\times$ 12 + 3 = psig

Convert 1-5 VDC to 4-20 mA
VDC - 1 ÷ 4 × 16 + 4 = mA

Convert 1-5 VDC to 3-15 psig
VDC - 1 ÷ 4 × 12 + 3 = psig

Convert 3-15 psig to 1-5 VDC
psig - 3 ÷ 12 × 4 + 1 = VDC

Convert 3-15 psig to 4-20 mA
psig - 3 ÷ 12 × 16 + 4 = mA

Example: 16 mA equals to what 3-15 psig signal?
 16 mA - 4 ÷ 16 × 12 + 3 = 12 psig
Example: 10 psig equals to what 4-20 mA signal?
 10 psig - 3 ÷ 12 × 16 + 4 = 13.3 mA

 Conversion Shortcut for 1-5 VDC and 4-20
mA signals **only**.

mA ÷ 4 = VDC or **VDC × 4 = mA**
Example: 12 mA ÷ 4 = 3 VDC
Example: 2 VDC × 4 = 8 mA

Process Related Formulas
Percentage Formula
[PV is Process Variable, LRV is Lower Range Variable & URV is Upper Range Variable]

% = (PV - LRV) ÷ (URV - LRV)

Example: What % is a PV of 160 GPM when the range is 0 to 200 GPM?

(160 - 0) ÷ (200 - 0) = .8 or 80%

PV and/or Signal Formula
[X is either the PV, a 4-20 mA or 1-5VDC]

X = %(URV - LRV) + LRV

Example#1: What mA signal equates to 90% of the transmitter range?

.9 (20 - 4) + (4) = 18.4 mA

Example #2: What PV equates to 65% of a -25 to 175°C range?

.65 (175) - (-25) + (-25) = 105°C

Example #3: What PV equates to 75% of a -25 to
175°C range?

.75 (175) - (-25) + (-25) = 125°C

X = (URV - LRV) % + LRV

Example#1: What mA signal equates to 90% of the transmitter range?

$(20 - 4)(.9) + (4) = 18.4$ mA

Example #2: What PV equates to 65% of a -25 to 175°C range?

$(175) - (-25)(.65) + (-25) = 105$°C

Example #3: What PV equates to 75% of a -25 to 175°C range?

$(175) - (-25)(.75) + (-25) = 125$°C

++++++++++++++++++++++++++++++++++

Use a "Stinger" for field calibration of D/P transmitters.

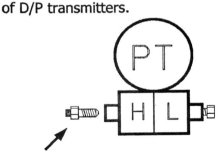

SPECIAL BLEEDER FITTING FOR CALIBRATING PRESSURE TRANSMITTERS IN THE FIELD.

NEMA and NEC Enclosure Types

National Electrical Manufacturers Association
NEMA Standards 1-10-1979.

Type Designation	Intended Use and Description
1	Enclosures are intended for indoor use primarily to provide a degree of protection against contact with the enclosed equipment.
2	Enclosures are intended for indoor use primarily to provide a degree of protection against limited amounts of falling water and dirt.
3	Enclosures are intended for outdoor use primarily to provide a degree of protection against windblown dust, rain, sleet, and external ice formation.
3R	Enclosures are intended for outdoor use primarily to provide a degree of protection against falling rain, sleet, and external ice formation.
4	Enclosures are intended for indoor or outdoor use primarily to provide a degree of protection against windblown dust and rain, splashing water, and hose-directed water.
4X	Enclosures are intended for indoor or outdoor use primarily to provide a degree of protection against corrosion, windblown dust and rain, splashing water, and hose-directed water.
6	Submersible, watertight, dusttight and sleet-(ice) resistant—indoor and outdoor. A type 6 enclosure is suitable for indoor and outdoor application where the equipment may be subject to occasional submersion, as in quarries, mines and manholes. The design of the enclosure will depend upon the specified conditions of pressure and time.
7	Class I (Groups A, B, C or D) Indoor Hazardous Locations—Air Break Equipment. Suitable for indoors, these enclosures are designed to meet the application requirement of the National Electrical Code for Class I hazardous locations which may be in effect from time to time. In this type of equipment, the circuit interruption occurs in air.
9	Class II (Groups E, F, or G) Indoor Hazardous Locations—Air Break Equipment. Suitable for indoors, these enclosures are designed to meet the application requirements of the National Electrical Code for Class II, Groups E, F and G locations.
12	Enclosures are intended for indoor use primarily to provide a degree of protection against dust, falling dirt, and dripping noncorrosive liquids.
13	Enclosures are intended for indoor use primarily to provide a degree of protection against dust, spraying of water, oil, and noncorrosive coolant.

The preceding descriptions are not intended to be complete representations of National Electric Manufacturers Association standards for enclosures.

OHM'S LAW / POWER FORMULAS

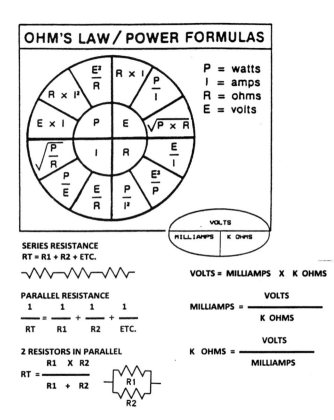

P = watts
I = amps
R = ohms
E = volts

SERIES RESISTANCE

$R_T = R_1 + R_2 + \text{ETC.}$

PARALLEL RESISTANCE

$$\frac{1}{R_T} = \frac{1}{R_1} + \frac{1}{R_2} + \frac{1}{\text{ETC.}}$$

2 RESISTORS IN PARALLEL

$$R_T = \frac{R_1 \times R_2}{R_1 + R_2}$$

VOLTS = MILLIAMPS $\times$ K OHMS

$$\text{MILLIAMPS} = \frac{\text{VOLTS}}{\text{K OHMS}}$$

$$\text{K OHMS} = \frac{\text{VOLTS}}{\text{MILLIAMPS}}$$

Color	Digit	Multiplier	Tolerance (%)
Black	0	10^0 (1)	
Brown	1	10^1	1
Red	2	10^2	2
Orange	3	10^3	
Yellow	4	10^4	
Green	5	10^5	0.5
Blue	6	10^6	0.25
Violet	7	10^7	0.1
Grey	8	10^8	
White	9	10^9	
Gold		10^{-1}	5
Silver		10^{-2}	10
(none)			20

Digit   Digit   Multiplier   Tolerance

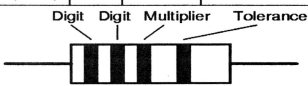

RESISTOR COLOR CODE

COMMON DCS FUSE SIZES (ballpark values only)

Analog Inputs	24VDC	1/8 amp
Analog Outputs	24VDC	1/4 amp
Digital Outputs	120VAC	Variable up to 2 amps
Digital Outputs	24VDC	Variable up to 2 amps
Digital Inputs	120VAC	1/4 amp
Digital Inputs	24VDC	1/4 amp

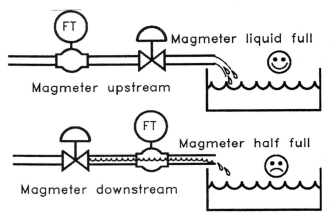

Magmeter liquid full

Magmeter upstream

Magmeter half full

Magmeter downstream

As a general rule all flowmeters should be installed upstream of their control valves. For gas and steam applications it helps the pressure to stay closer to the design pressure as well as reducing inlet turbulence. When flowmeters are after the control valve, turbulence can reduce measurement accuracy. Shown above are two examples of a horizontal liquid flow discharging to atmosphere. When magmeters (and other flowmeters) are located downstream, the process liquid might only partially fill it thus giving measurement errors.

$$\text{\% OF ACCURACY (ERROR)} = \frac{\triangle \text{ IN READINGS}}{\text{FULL SCALE SPAN}} \times 100$$

TRUE PROCESS PRESSURE = 115 PSIG
TRANSMITTER RANGE = 0−200 PSIG
READING OF TRANSMITTER = 118 PSIG

$$\text{\% OF ACCURACY (ERROR)} = \frac{118-115}{200} \times 100$$

% OF ACCURACY (ERROR) = 1.5%

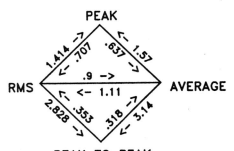

AC VOLTAGE FORMULAS

PUSH BUTTONS

MOMENTARY CONTACT					MAINTAINED CONTACT	
SINGLE CIRCUIT		DOUBLE CIRCUIT	MUSHROOM HEAD	WOBBLE STICK	TWO SINGLE CKT.	ONE DOUBLE CKT.
N.O.	N.C.	N.O. & N.C.				

TIMED CONTACTS - CONTACT ACTION RETARDED AFTER COIL IS:

ENERGIZED		DE-ENERGIZED	
N.O.T.C.	N.C.T.O.	N.O.T.O.	N.C.T.C.

FOOT SWITCHES

N.O.	N.C.

LIMIT SWITCHES

NORMALLY OPEN	NORMALLY CLOSED
HELD CLOSED	HELD OPEN

42

PRESSURE & VACUUM SWITCHES		LIQUID LEVEL SWITCH	
N.O.	N.C.	N.O.	N.C.

TEMPERATURE ACTUATED SWITCH		FLOW SWITCH (AIR, WATER, ETC.)	
N.O.	N.C.	N.O.	N.C.

SWITCH & RELAY CONTACTS

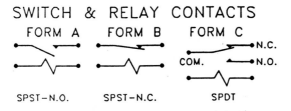

FORM A   FORM B   FORM C

N.C.

COM.   N.O.

SPST-N.O.   SPST-N.C.   SPDT

43

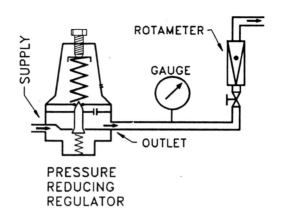

PRESSURE
REDUCING
REGULATOR

PRESSURE REDUCING REGULATORS

The best method to set pressure reducing regulators is in
the field under actual operating conditions. If you need
25 psig, simply adjust the knob on the top until you get
that output pressure. The test hook-up shown above
simulates the field flow conditions with a rotameter. It
is good only if you know the flow rate required. There
could be an error if you set the regulator without using
the operating flow rate. This is because as flow through
the regulator increases, the regulated output will tend
to "Droop" or decrease.

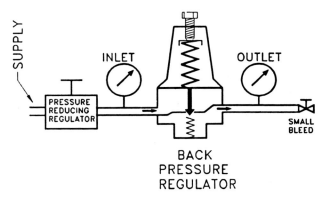

**BACK
PRESSURE
REGULATOR**

BACK PRESSURE REGULATOR

A back pressure regulator operates like an adjustable relief valve. That is, it will begin to open only when the upstream pressure exceeds the set value. Suppose we wanted to set a back pressure regulator to 35 psig. Hook up the back pressure regulator as shown in the drawing. Set the input test pressure to the desired pressure, 35 psig in this case. Increase the back pressure regulator setting until pressure (any amount) starts showing on the discharge test gauge. Decrease the input test pressure slightly (maybe down to 32 psig) so that the discharge pressure bleeds off. Test it by SLOWLY increasing the input test pressure again up to 35 psig and see if pressure again shows on the discharge gauge. Adjust and repeat as necessary to get the back pressure regulator to just start discharging pressure when you apply 35 psig to the inlet.

DVMM = Digital Volt Multimeter
DVOM = Digital Volt Ohm Meter

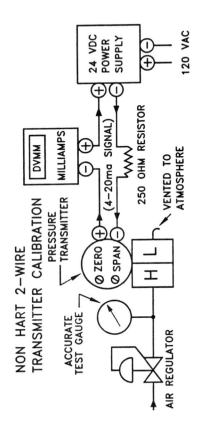

NON HART 2-WIRE
TRANSMITTER CALIBRATION

Differential Pressure Transmitter Calibration
(no elevation or suppression) 3-point check

To calibrate a D/P transmitter for a range of 0 to 30 inches of water (" H2O), you will need a 24 VDC power supply, a mA meter, an air pressure reducing regulator, an accurate test gauge or manometer and a 250 ohm resistor hooked in series as shown.

Step 1   Connect all of the wires and tubing as shown. The low pressure side of the D/P transmitter should be vented.

Step 2   Test all calibration points by approaching them both upscale and downscale. Apply 0, 50, 100, 50 and 0 percent of the range. In our example it would be 0, 15, 30, 15 and 0 inches of water. Record the output values "as found" at each calibration point and calculate the percent of error.

Step 3   Again apply 0 inches of water to the high pressure side of the transmitter. If the DVMM does not read exactly 4 mA of current, adjust the zero screw to obtain it.

Step 4   Apply 30 inches of water to the high pressure side of the transmitter. If the DVMM does not read 20 mA adjust the span screw until it does.

Step 5   Repeat steps 3 and 4 until there is no error.

Step 6   Check the calibration in the middle (50%) of the range at 15" H2O. If there is an error and the transmitter has a linearity adjustment, make a correction. Repeat steps 2, 3 and, 4 to bring the transmitter into proper calibration. If it won't calibrate, repair or replace the transmitter.

Step 7   The final calibration check should be for all calibration points from 0 to 30 inches of water and back down to zero again as you did in step 2. Document the values at all points. The calibration is now complete.

Notes

* Since regulators may leak slightly, it is best to vent the high pressure side of the transmitter to atmosphere rather than to use the regulator for the zero value.

* Usually the "as found" and the final calibration output values are documented on the calibration sheet. To find the percent of error, divide the difference between the "as found" output value and the correct output value by the output span (16 in this case.) Then multiply by 100. As an example, suppose the "as found" value was 12.2 mA when the correct value is 12 mA. Therefore .2 divided by 16, times 100 is an error of 1.25%.

* When calibrating with analog devices such as pressure regulators and temperature baths, each calibration point must be approached slowly without overshooting it. Because of the effects of hysteresis, it is necessary to slowly approach each calibration pressure point from below it and from above it.

* Use the following formulas to determine the analog output (4-20 mA) signal or the inches of water input value for any point.

* Often the acceptable percent of error (accuracy) tolerances for the process instruments is +/- 1.0% of span. Usually the test equipment will have at least four time the accuracy of the instrument being calibrated.

$$\text{Output signal (4-20 mA)} = \frac{\text{inches of water}}{\text{Max inches of water Range}} \times (16) - 4$$

$$\text{Inches of water} = \frac{\text{mA} - 4}{16} \times \text{Max inches of water Range}$$

$$\% \text{ of Error} = \frac{(\text{As Found Output}) - (\text{Correct Output})}{\text{Output Span}} \times 100$$

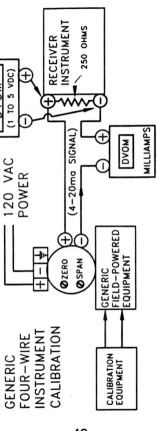

GENERIC FOUR–WIRE INSTRUMENT CALIBRATION

RECEIVER INSTRUMENT

250 OHMS

DVOM (1 TO 5 VDC)

DVOM

MILLIAMPS

120 VAC POWER

(4–20ma SIGNAL)

ZERO

SPAN

GENERIC FIELD–POWERED EQUIPMENT

CALIBRATION EQUIPMENT

Vacuum Transmitter Calibration

Hook up the vacuum transmitter as shown. The vacuum is regulated by adjusting the bleed valve. Make sure that there are no tubing leaks. The example shown has a range of 0-150 inches of water absolute. Since the manometer must be connected in reverse, convert the terms of inches of water vacuum by using the proper formula. Some manometers use mercury yet are marked in inches of water column. Values near absolute zero are impossible to obtain with a vacuum pump. You may want to pick a value near it as your zero point for calibration purposes.

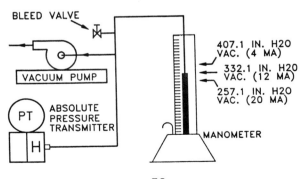

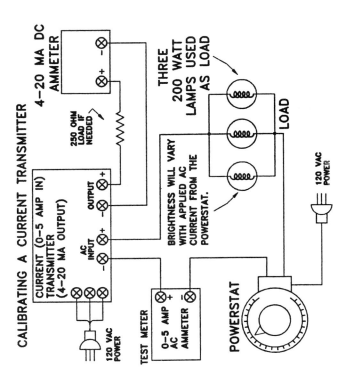

CALIBRATING A CURRENT TRANSMITTER

4-20 MA DC AMMETER

250 OHM LOAD IF NEEDED

THREE 200 WATT LAMPS USED AS LOAD

LOAD

BRIGHTNESS WILL VARY WITH APPLIED AC CURRENT FROM THE POWERSTAT.

120 VAC POWER

CURRENT (0-5 AMP IN) TRANSMITTER (4-20 MA OUTPUT)

OUTPUT

AC INPUT

120 VAC POWER

TEST METER

0-5 AMP AC AMMETER

POWERSTAT

LEVEL CALCULATION
EXAMPLES

STATIC HEAD TYPE LEVEL CALCULATIONS

Two main things have to be considered with static
head level measurements; the range of the transmitter and
the elevation or suppression forces. Elevation is
compensation for unwanted forces on the low pressure
connection of the level transmitter. Suppression is
compensation for unwanted forces on the high pressure
connection. Notice the typical example following.

1. Determine the span in inches of water (also called
   inches of water column [inches of W.C.] or " H2O) by
   multiplying the distance between the measurement taps
   and the specific gravity of the process fluid. 45
   inches times .98 equals 44.1 inches of water. Since
   the span is 44.1 " H2O that means the range is equal
   to 0 to 44.1 " H2O.
2. Next determine the effects of any elevation or
   suppression. Since the transmitter is mounted even
   with the lower tap (the 0% point), there is no
   suppression to consider. However, in this case a seal
   fluid of 1.2 specific gravity is used, therefore
   elevation must be considered. To determine the
   elevation multiply the height of the seal leg times
   the seal fluid specific gravity. 45 inches times 1.2
   equals 54 inches of water.

* The calibration becomes: Range = 0 to 44.1 " H2O
                            Elevation = 54 " H2O

NOTE When you have both elevation and suppression
forces, they may cancel or partially cancel out each
other. If they are not equal, subtract the lesser from
the greater (usually elevation is the greater) and
calibrate the transmitter using the difference of the
greater force.

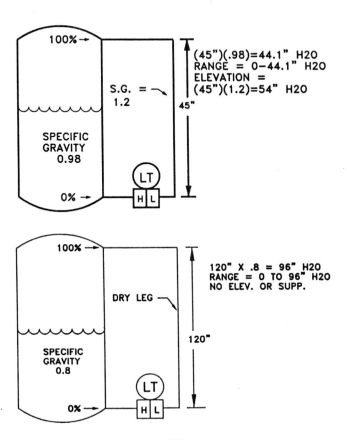

100% →

(45")(.98)=44.1" H2O
RANGE = 0−44.1" H2O
ELEVATION =
(45")(1.2)=54" H2O

S.G. = 1.2

45"

SPECIFIC GRAVITY 0.98

0% →

LT
H L

100% →

DRY LEG

120" X .8 = 96" H2O
RANGE = 0 TO 96" H2O
NO ELEV. OR SUPP.

120"

SPECIFIC GRAVITY 0.8

0% →

LT
H L

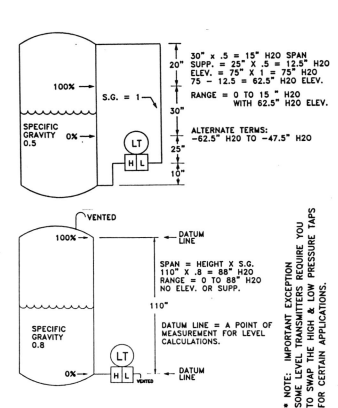

30" x .5 = 15" H2O SPAN
SUPP. = 25" X .5 = 12.5" H2O
ELEV. = 75" X 1 = 75" H2O
75 - 12.5 = 62.5" H2O ELEV.

RANGE = 0 TO 15 " H2O
WITH 62.5" H2O ELEV.

ALTERNATE TERMS:
-62.5" H2O TO -47.5" H2O

SPAN = HEIGHT X S.G.
110" X .8 = 88" H2O
RANGE = 0 TO 88" H2O
NO ELEV. OR SUPP.

DATUM LINE = A POINT OF
MEASUREMENT FOR LEVEL
CALCULATIONS.

* NOTE: IMPORTANT EXCEPTION
SOME LEVEL TRANSMITERS REQUIRE YOU
TO SWAP THE HIGH & LOW PRESSURE TAPS
FOR CERTAIN APPLICATIONS.

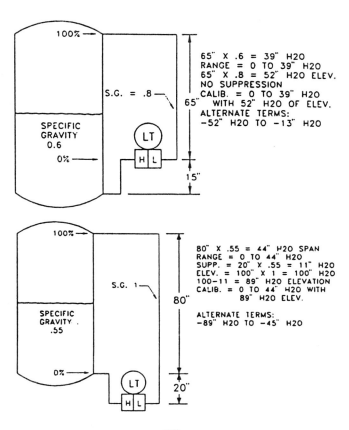

65" X .6 = 39" H2O
RANGE = 0 TO 39" H2O
65" X .8 = 52" H2O ELEV.
NO SUPPRESSION
CALIB. = 0 TO 39" H2O
   WITH 52" H2O OF ELEV.
ALTERNATE TERMS:
-52" H2O TO -13" H2O

100% →
S.G. = .8
65"
SPECIFIC
GRAVITY
0.6
0% →
LT
H | L
15"

80" X .55 = 44" H2O SPAN
RANGE = 0 TO 44" H2O
SUPP. = 20" X .55 = 11" H2O
ELEV. = 100" X 1 = 100" H2O
100-11 = 89" H2O ELEVATION
CALIB. = 0 TO 44" H2O WITH
   89" H2O ELEV.

ALTERNATE TERMS:
-89" H2O TO -45" H2O

100% →
S.G. 1
80"
SPECIFIC
GRAVITY
.55
0% →
LT
H | L
20"

55

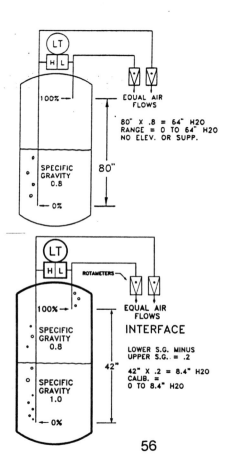

EQUAL AIR
FLOWS

80" X .8 = 64" H2O
RANGE = 0 TO 64" H2O
NO ELEV. OR SUPP.

100%

SPECIFIC
GRAVITY
0.8

80"

0%

ROTAMETERS

EQUAL AIR
FLOWS

INTERFACE

LOWER S.G. MINUS
UPPER S.G. = .2

42" X .2 = 8.4" H2O
CALIB. =
0 TO 8.4" H2O

100%

SPECIFIC
GRAVITY
0.8

SPECIFIC
GRAVITY
1.0

42"

0%

56

CONTROLLER ACTION

Most control loops use negative feedback to keep the process variable (PV) at the set point value. In other words, if the PV drifts in one direction, the controller will give a corrective signal to force it to move back in the opposite direction. The best way to determine the proper controller action is to start with a PV increase. See the control loop example below. If the PV (flow in this case) increases, the reverse acting controller would send a decreasing signal to the control valve. Less air to the A/O (air to open) valve will tend to close it. When the control valve closes, it will reduce the flow. With less flow, the PV reduces back to the set point. The controller has the correct action.

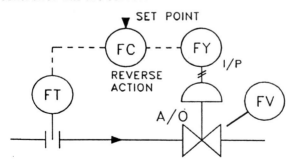

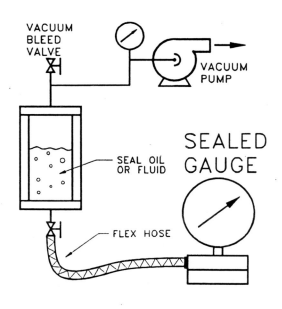

VACUUM
BLEED
VALVE

VACUUM
PUMP

SEALED
GAUGE

SEAL OIL
OR FLUID

FLEX HOSE

Sealing Gauges and Instruments

Notice the attached drawing with a diaphragm seal pressure gauge. You will need an oil reservoir, a vacuum pump with a gauge, a metal flexible hose and the necessary tubing and valve fittings. Hook up the device as shown in the drawing. To add the seal fluid (oil in this case), block the vacuum bleed valve and turn on the vacuum pump. You will notice the oil vigorously bubbling in the reservoir. After the most vacuum has been obtained, turn off the pump and open the vacuum bleed valve to remove the vacuum on the system. Turn and orient the gauge in every direction necessary to allow all the air bubbles to float and find their way out. Again block the vacuum bleed valve and turn on the vacuum pump. Repeat the procedure above of applying vacuum and allowing the oil to drain back into the gauge until there is virtually no bubbling in the reservoir. You might have to repeat the procedure 4 or 6 times. The gauge should end up liquid full without any air pockets. To remove the flex hose, keep the connection of the gauge upward so that none of the sealing oil can drain out. Carefully remove the flex hose then plug the connection to the gauge. Now the gauge will need to be recalibrated.

OPEN LOOP PNEUMATIC CONTROLLER ALIGNMENT CHECKS (3-15 PSIG SYSTEM)

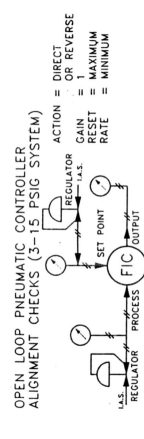

ACTION = DIRECT OR REVERSE

GAIN = 1
RESET = MAXIMUM
RATE = MINIMUM

CONNECT THE CONTROLLER TO BE ALIGNED AS SHOWN.

After placing the set point and process together anywhere on the scale:
1. The output should be 9 psig.
2. The gain can be changed without an output change.
3. The action of the controller can be changed without an output change. (This is not true for all models.)

60

CLOSED LOOP PNEUMATIC CONTROLLER ALIGNMENT CHECKS

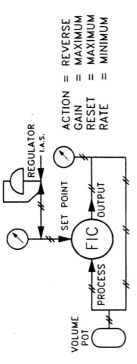

ACTION = REVERSE
GAIN = MAXIMUM
RESET = MAXIMUM
RATE = MINIMUM

CONNECT THE CONTROLLER TO BE ALIGNED AS SHOWN.

The set point and process will track (since they are tied together) 3 to 15 psig. With the set point anywhere on the scale:

1. The gain can be changed without an output change.
2. The action can be changed without an output change. (This is not true for all models)

Special Controller Alignment

Local controllers that use process forces such as pressure or temperature instead of a 3-15 psig input signal can be checked for proper alignment by using an open loop method. Use the example of the Wizard pressure controller shown in the drawing. The input range is 0-150 psig. Set the gain to 1 and the reset to a fast setting such as .005 M/R (minutes per repeat). Place the set point to mid-scale (75 psig) and apply half of the process pressure (75 psig). Adjust the nozzle for a 9 psig (50%) output signal. Reduce the set point to 10% (15 psig) of the process. The output should again have a 9 psig signal. Increase the set point to 90% of scale and apply 90% of the process (135 psig). Verify that the output signal again shows 9 psig. If the output signal was not fairly close to 9 psig, the nozzle assembly may need to be adjusted for better alignment.

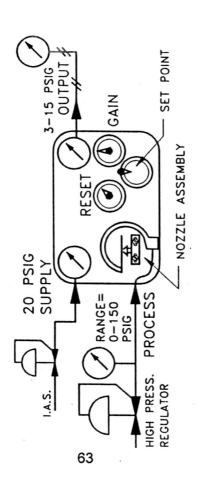

3-15 PSIG OUTPUT

GAIN

SET POINT

RESET

NOZZLE ASSEMBLY

20 PSIG SUPPLY

I.A.S.

RANGE= 0-150 PSIG

PROCESS

HIGH PRESS. REGULATOR

Helpful Pipe Flange Information

Series 150 Flange

Pipe Size	Wrench Size	Flange Bolts		Raised Face				Ring Joint	
		Quan.	Size	Stud L'gth	Gasket I.D.	Gasket O.D.	Flange Dia.	Stud L'gth	Ring No.
1	7/8	4	1/2	2-1/2	1	2-5/8	4-1/4	3	R15
1-1/2	7/8	4	1/2	2-3/4		3-3/8	5	3-1/4	R19
2	1-1/16	4	5/8	3-1/4	1-1/2	4-1/2	6	3-3/4	R22
3	1-1/16	4	5/8	3-1/2	3	5-3/8	7-1/2	4-1/4	R29
4	1-1/16	8	5/8	3-1/2	4	6-7/8	9	4-1/4	R36
6	1-1/4	8	3/4	4	6	8-3/4	11	4-1/2	R43
8	1-1/4	8	3/4	4-1/4	8	11	13-1/2	4-3/4	R48
10	1-7/16	12	7/8	4-3/4	10	13-3/8	16	5-1/4	R52
12	1-7/16	12	7/8	4-3/4	12	16-1/8	19	5-1/2	R56
14	1-5/8	12	1	5-1/4	13-1/4	17-3/4	21	6	R59
16	1-5/8	16	1	5-1/2	15-1/4	20-1/4	23-1/2	6	R64
18	1-13/16	16	1-1/8	6	17-1/4	21-5/8	25	6-1/2	R68
20	1-13/16	20	1-1/8	6-1/4	19-1/4	23-7/8	27-1/2	7	R72
24	2	20	1-1/4	7	23-1/4	28-1/4	32	7-3/4	R76

Series 300 Flange

| Pipe Size | Wrench Size | Flange Bolts | | Stud L'gth | Raised Face | | Flange Dia. | Ring Joint | |
| | | Quan. | Size | | Gasket | | | Stud L'gth | Ring No. |
					I.D.	O.D.			
1	1-1/16	4	5/8	3	1	2-7/8	4-7/8	3-1/4	R16
1-1/2	1-1/4	4	3/4	3-1/2	1-1/2	3-3/4	6-1/8	4	R20
2	1-1/16	8	5/8	3-1/2	2	4-3/8	6-1/2	4-1/4	R23
3	1-1/4	8	3/4	4-1/4	3	5-7/8	8-1/4	5	R31
4	1-1/4	8	3/4	4-1/2	4	7-1/2	10	5-1/4	R37
6	1-1/4	12	3/4	4-3/4	6	9-7/8	12-1/2	5-3/4	R45
8	1-7/16	12	7/8	5-1/2	8	12-1/8	15	6-1/4	R49
10	1-5/8	16	1	6-1/4	10	14-1/4	17-1/2	7-1/4	R53
12	1-13/16	16	1-1/2	6-3/4	12	16-5/8	20-1/2	7-1/2	R57
14	1-13/16	20	1-1/8	7	13-1/4	19-1/8	23	7-3/4	R61
16	2	20	1-1/8	7-1/2	15-1/4	21-1/4	25-1/2	8-1/2	R65
18	2	24	1-1/4	7-3/4	17	23-1/2	28	8-1/4	R69
20	2	24	1-1/4	8-1/4	19	25-3/4	30-1/2	9-1/4	R73
24	2-3/8	24	1-1/2	9-1/4	23	30-1/2	36	10-1/4	R77

Series 600 Flange

Pipe Size	Wrench Size	Flange Bolts		Raised Face				Ring Joint	
		Quan.	Size	Stud L'gth	Gasket I.D.	Gasket O.D.	Flange Dia.	Stud L'gth	Ring No.
1	1-1/16	4	5/8	3-1/2	1-5/16	2-7/8	4-7/8	3-1/2	R16
1-1/2	1-1/4	4	3/4	4-1/4	1-29/32	3-3/4	6-1/8	4-1/4	R20
2	1-1/16	8	5/8	4-1/4	2	4-3/8	6-1/2	4-1/2	R23
3	1-1/4	8	3/4	5	3	5-7/8	8-1/4	5-1/4	R31
4	1-7/16	8	7/8	5-3/4	4	7-5/8	10-3/4	6	R37
6	1-5/8	12	1	6-3/4	6	10-1/2	14	7	R45
8	1-13/16	12	1-1/8	7-3/4	7-7/8	12-5/8	16-1/2	8	R49
10	2	16	1-1/4	8-1/2	9-3/4	15-3/4	20	8-3/4	R53
12	2	20	1-1/4	8-3/4	11-3/4	18	22	9	R57
14	2-3/16	20	1-3/8	9-1/4	12-7/8	19-3/8	23-3/4	9-1/2	R61
16	2-3/8	20	1-1/2	10	14-3/4	22-1/4	27	10-1/4	R65
18	2-9/16	20	1-5/8	10-3/4	16-1/2	24-1/8	29-1/4	11	R69
20	2-9/16	24	1-5/8	11-1/2	18-1/4	26-7/8	32	11-3/4	R73
24	2-15/16	24	1-7/8	13	22	31-1/8	37	13-1/2	R77

Controller Tuning Information

10% Proportional Band (P.B.) = fast = narrow band
200% Proportional Band (P.B.) = slow = wide band
10 Gain = fast action
.1 Gain = slow action

$$\text{Gain} = \frac{\text{Change in Output}}{\text{Change in Input}} \qquad \text{Gain} = \frac{100}{\%\text{P.B.}}$$

$$\%\text{ P.B.} = \frac{100}{\text{Gain}} \qquad \%\text{ P.B.} = \frac{\text{Change in Input}}{\text{Change in Output}} \times 100$$

Minutes/Repeat (M/R)   Repeats /Minute (R/M)
.1 M/R = Fast   .1 R/M = Slow
10 M/R = Slow   10 R/M = Fast

Derivative (Pre-Act, Rate)
0 Minutes of Lead Time = No Derivative action
20 Minutes of Lead Time = Lots of Deriv. action

INITIAL CONTROLLER SETTINGS

	Gain	Reset (M/R)	Deriv.
Flow	.7	.1	-
Pressure	1.0	.2	-
Temp. (slow)	1.5	5.0	1.0 minute
Temp. (fast)	0.5	5.0	-
Level (slow)	2.0	4.0	-
Level (fast)	1.0	20.0	-
Analyzer (slow)	0.7	30.0	-

These initial controller settings are only a good starting place. Adjustments will be needed to obtain the best response that most loops can achieve. The 1/4 decay waveform shown below is the best response that most loops can achieve.

Too much loop gain causes continuous cycling of the process variable. Too little loop gain causes the process variable to wander. Too much reset action (.1 M/R) will cause continuous cycling. Too little reset action will cause an OFFSET between the set point and the process variable. Very few loops ever benefit from derivative action, use it sparingly.

* When tuning cascade loops, tune the slave first by itself. Have the master loop in manual. Tune the salve so that rapid set point changes do not cause it to go into oscillations. With that done, place the loop back into cascade control. Now tune only the master loop keeping in mind that the strength of the reset action of both the master and salve loops tend to be multiplied. In other words, a little reset action in the master loop will go a long way.

The Bump and Watch Tuning Method.

For a proportional and reset controller using gain and reset in minutes per repeat (M/R).

1)   Line out the controller in manual mode. If it will not reasonably line out in manual, it will be difficult to tune.

2)   Change settings to make it a proportional only controller. (No reset or rate) Try a robust gain initial setting of about 4 or more.

3)   If the process starts cycling continuously, decrease the gain enough to make it stop.

4)   In Automatic mode and process not cycling, increase the gain by about 50% of its reading. (A .25 gain would increase to .375 gain.)

5)   Make a 10% change (bump) in the set point and watch the process variable (PV) to see if it starts cycling. Give it time to react. Start with a 10% set point bump upward. Next time bump it 10% downward. That would bring it back to the original setting. Alternate the bump actions to keep the set point in the general area.

6)   If necessary, keep increasing the gain reading by 50% and bumping the set point until the process variable cycles continuously.

7)   Once you have cycling, set the gain at half of the last reading just before it started cycling.

8)   With the gain set, add 4 M/R of reset. Bump the set point and watch for continuous cycling.

9)   If no PV cycling, cut reset time in half (2 M/R) then bump and watch again. Repeat this until you do have continuous cycling. Set the rest at twice the last setting where the PV did not cycle.

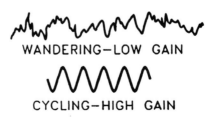

WANDERING—LOW GAIN

CYCLING—HIGH GAIN

SAFETY TIP

Never take someone's word that an instrument has been depressured properly. Carefully test it yourself.

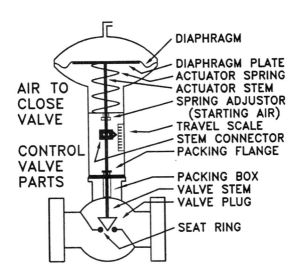

DIAPHRAGM
DIAPHRAGM PLATE
ACTUATOR SPRING
ACTUATOR STEM
SPRING ADJUSTOR
(STARTING AIR)
TRAVEL SCALE
STEM CONNECTOR
PACKING FLANGE
PACKING BOX
VALVE STEM
VALVE PLUG
SEAT RING

AIR TO
CLOSE
VALVE

CONTROL
VALVE
PARTS

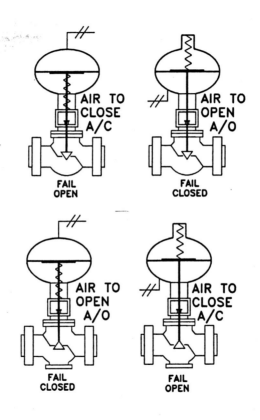

AIR TO
CLOSE
A/C

**FAIL
OPEN**

AIR TO
OPEN
A/O

**FAIL
CLOSED**

AIR TO
OPEN
A/O

**FAIL
CLOSED**

AIR TO
CLOSE
A/C

**FAIL
OPEN**

72

BENCH SETTING A CONTROL VALVE

After a valve has been overhauled or disassembled, the bench set should be properly adjusted.

TO BENCH SET AN AIR TO OPEN VALVE (for 3-15 psig)

1. With the plug stem disconnected from the actuator, adjust the starting air so that the actuator stem begins to move at 3.25 psig. Check the actuator to ensure that it will travel 100% with 3 to 15 psig applied. The travel indicator should agree at 0, 25, 75 and 100% of travel. Apply an increasing then decreasing signal in order to test for hysteresis, which should not exceed 1/4 psig.
2. With the valve plug in the closed position and 3 psig applied to the actuator, connect the valve and actuator stems together.
3. Stroke the valve by applying 3-15 psig to the actuator. It should smoothly travel over its entire range. The valve should be tightly closed at 3 psig. Check the total valve hysteresis to make sure that it does not exceed 1/4 psig.

BENCH SET FOR AIR TO CLOSE VALVE (3-15 psig)

1. With the plug stem disconnected from the actuator, adjust the starting air so that the actuator stem begins to move at 3 psig. Check the actuator to ensure that it will travel 100% with 3 to 15 psig applied. The travel indicator should agree at 0, 25, 75 and 100% of travel. Apply an increasing then decreasing signal in order to test for hysteresis, which should not exceed 1/4 psig.
2. With the valve plug in the closed position and with 14.75 psig applied to the actuator, connect the valve and actuator stems together.
3. Stroke the valve by applying 3-15 psig to the actuator. It should smoothly travel over its entire range. The valve should be tightly closed at 15 psig. Check the total valve hysteresis to make sure that it does not exceed 1/4 psig.

Valve Leakage Test   One method to determine the approximate amount of leakage in a control valve is to cover the outlet connection with a wet paper towel. The water will allow the paper to adhere and form a seal. With the actuator in the closed position, apply about 20 psig of air to the inlet port. With zero leakage, the wet paper towel will maintain its seal. Small amounts of leakage will bubble up and break the seal occasionally. When you have excessive leakage, you will not be able to keep the seal formed very long.

Standard Bench Set Most control valves have a standard bench set of 3-15 psig. You can also find 6-30 psig used as a standard too, but not as often. When process differential pressures act upon a valve plug, they either tend to help the valve open or tend to help it close. When a small actuator is chosen, (usually for economic reasons) its bench set will have to be non-standard in order to compensate for the pressures.

Bench set for Air to Open (5-15 psig) When process conditions force you to purchase valves with a non-standard bench set, such as 5-15 psig, the valve will have a specific range spring. That is why the span is 10 psig instead of the usual 3-15 psig. Differential pressure across the valve trim is compensated by the non-standard bench set. When such a valve is placed in the actual process, it will stroke approximately 3-15 psig.   If adjusted correctly, the valve will be closed at 5 psig, half open at 10 psig and fully open with 15 psig applied. Non-standard bench settings such as this one are used to overcome process pressures that tend to open the valve. If you desire to have a 3-15 psig bench set, you must purchase a larger actuator which can exert more force.

SPLIT RANGE BENCH SET (3-9 PSIG A/O)

Split range and sequencing bench sets are done in similar fashion like the two examples above. If a valve positioner is to be used, bench set the valve first, then add the positioner.

Split Range Options

When a typical 3-9 psig and 9-15 psig split range system is needed, there are several ways to accomplish it.

1) Use two valves with spring ranges of 3-9 psig and 9-15 psig.

2) Use two valves with normal 3-15 psig spring ranges. Equip one with a positioner so that an input of 3-9 psig will give an output air signal of 3-15 psig. Equip the other one with a positioner so that an input of 9-15 psig will give an output signal of 3-15 psig.

3) Use two valves with normal 3-15 psig spring ranges but use pneumatic signal conditioners that will take 3-9 psig and 9-15 psig as input signals and give 3-15 psig as an output.

4) Use two normal 3-15 psig valves with individual output signals from the DCS. Configure the DCS system to do the split range.

Safety Tip

Never add stem packing to a control valve while it is in service and under pressure. It could easily blow out product and cause an injury.

CONTROL VALVE MAX. LEAKAGE RATINGS

Class I   no test required

Class II   .5% of valve capacity, air at 50 psid

Class III   .1% of valve capacity, air at 50 psid

Class IV .01% of valve capacity, air at 50 psid

Class V   .0005 ml per minute of water per inch
                of port diameter per psi differential.
                (water at service differential pressure)

Class VI   Air tested at service diff. or 50 psid

PORT DIAM.	BUBBLES/MIN.
1 inch	1
1-1/2 inch	2
2 inch	3
2-1/2 inch	4
3 inch	6
4 inch	11
6 inch	27
8 inch	45

TUBE IN
1" OF WATER

TEST
PRESSURE

VALVE SIZING FORMULAS

CRITICAL FLOW IS WHEN THE PRESSURE DROP EQUALS OR EXCEEDS ONE–HALF OF THE ABSOLUTE INLET PRESSURE.

SUBCRITICAL FLOW IS WHEN THE PRESSURE DROP IS LESS THAN ONE–HALF OF THE ABSOLUTE INLET PRESSURE.

CRITICAL AND SUBCRITICAL ARE TERMS THAT RELATE ONLY TO GAS OR STEAM SIZING FORMULAS.

LIQUID FLOW SIZING EQUATIONS

$$C_v = V\sqrt{\frac{G}{\Delta P}}$$

$$V = C_v\sqrt{\frac{\Delta P}{G}}$$

$$\Delta P = G\left(\frac{V}{C_v}\right)^2$$

C_v = VALVE FLOW COEFFICIENT
ΔP = PRESS. DROP @ MAX FLOW, PSI
G = SPECIFIC GRAVITY @ FLOW TEMP.
V = GPM @ FLOWING TEMPERATURE

GAS FLOW SIZING EQUATIONS

SUBCRITICAL FLOW

$$Cv = \frac{Q}{963} \sqrt{\frac{GTa}{\triangle P(P1+P2)}}$$

$$Q = 963\ Cv \sqrt{\frac{\triangle P(P1+P2)}{GTa}}$$

$$\triangle P = P1 - \sqrt{P1^2 - \left(\frac{Q\ \sqrt{GTa}}{963Cv}\right)^2}$$

CRITICAL FLOW

$$Q = \frac{835\ Cv\ P1}{\sqrt{GTa}}$$

$$Cv = \frac{Q\ \sqrt{GTa}}{835\ P1}$$

Cv = VALVE FLOW COEFFICIENT
$\triangle$P = PRESS. DROP ⊙ MAX FLOW, PSI
G = SPECIFIC GRAVITY ⊙ FLOW TEMP.
Q = SCFH FLOW ⊙ 14.7PSIA & 60 °F
P1 = INLET PRESS. ⊙ MAX FLOW, PSIA
P2 = OUTLET PRESS. ⊙ MAX FLOW, PSIA
Ta = ABSOLUTE TEMP. (460+ °F)

STEAM FLOW SIZING EQUATIONS

SUBCRITICAL FLOW

$$Cv = \frac{W(1+0.0007\ S)}{2.12\ \sqrt{\Delta P(P1+P2)}}$$

$$W = \frac{2.12\ Cv\ \sqrt{\Delta P(P1+P2)}}{1 + 0.0007\ S}$$

$$\Delta P = P1 - \sqrt{P1^2 - \left(\frac{W(1+0.0007\ S)}{2.12\ Cv}\right)^2}$$

CRITICAL FLOW

$$W = \frac{1.84\ Cv\ P1}{(1+0.0007\ S)}$$

$$Cv = \frac{W(1+0.0007\ S)}{1.84\ P1}$$

Cv = VALVE FLOW COEFFICIENT
ΔP = PRESS. DROP @ MAX FLOW, PSI
W = LB./HOUR
S = DEGREES OF SUPERHEAT
P1 = INLET PRESS. @ MAX FLOW, PSIA
P2 = OUTLET PRESS. @ MAX FLOW, PSIA

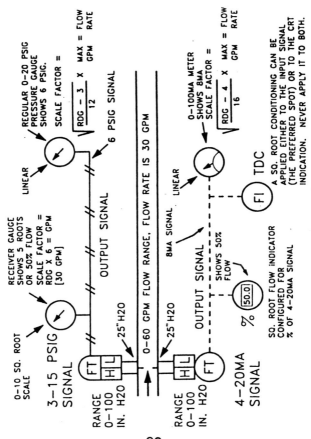

REGULAR 0-20 PSIG PRESSURE GAUGE SHOWS 6 PSIG.

SCALE FACTOR =

$$\sqrt{\dfrac{RDG - 3}{12}} \times MAX = \dfrac{FLOW}{GPM} \dfrac{RATE}{}$$

LINEAR

6 PSIG SIGNAL

OUTPUT SIGNAL

0-60 GPM FLOW RANGE, FLOW RATE IS 30 GPM

RECEIVER GAUGE SHOWS 5 ROOTS OR 50% FLOW

SCALE FACTOR = RDG X 6 = GPM
[30 GPM]

25"H2O

25"H2O

0-10 SQ. ROOT SCALE

3-15 PSIG SIGNAL

RANGE 0-100 IN. H2O

FT   HiL

0-100MA METER SHOWS 8MA
SCALE FACTOR =

$$\sqrt{\dfrac{RDG - 4}{16}} \times MAX = \dfrac{FLOW}{GPM} \dfrac{RATE}{}$$

LINEAR

FI   TDC

A SQ. ROOT CONDITIONING CAN BE APPLIED EITHER TO THE INPUT SIGNAL (THE PREFERRED SPOT) OR TO THE CRT INDICATION. NEVER APPLY IT TO BOTH.

8MA SIGNAL

LINEAR

OUTPUT SIGNAL

SHOWS 50% FLOW

50.0

%

SQ. ROOT FLOW INDICATOR CONFIGURED FOR % OF 4-20MA SIGNAL

4-20MA SIGNAL

RANGE 0-100 IN. H2O

HiL   FT

80

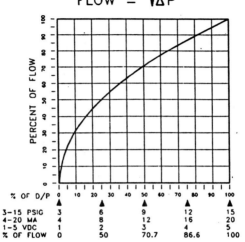

FLOW Vs DIFF. PRESSURE
FLOW = $\sqrt{\Delta P}$

% OF D/P	0				50			80		100
3-15 PSIG	3				6		9		12	15
4-20 MA	4				8		12		16	20
1-5 VDC	1				2		3		4	5
% OF FLOW	0				50		70.7		86.6	100

Square Root Signals

100% Flow	20.0 ma	15 psig	5.0 Volts
75%	13.0	9.75	3.25
50%	8.0	6.0	2.0
25%	5.0	3.75	1.25
0%	4.0	3.0	1.0

SQUARE ROOT FLOW FORMULAS

3-15 PSIG SIGNALS

$$\left(\frac{\text{FLOW RATE}}{\text{MAX. FLOW}}\right)^2 \times 12 + 3 = \begin{array}{l}\text{OUTPUT SIGNAL}\\\text{(3-15 PSIG)}\end{array}$$

$$\sqrt{\frac{\text{OUTPUT SIGNAL} - 3}{12}} \times \begin{array}{l}\text{MAX}\\\text{FLOW}\end{array} = \begin{array}{l}\text{FLOW}\\\text{RATE}\end{array}$$

4-20 MA SIGNALS

$$\left(\frac{\text{FLOW RATE}}{\text{MAX. FLOW}}\right)^2 \times 16 + 4 = \begin{array}{l}\text{OUTPUT SIGNAL}\\\text{(4-20 MA)}\end{array}$$

$$\sqrt{\frac{\text{OUTPUT SIGNAL} - 4}{16}} \times \begin{array}{l}\text{MAX}\\\text{FLOW}\end{array} = \begin{array}{l}\text{FLOW}\\\text{RATE}\end{array}$$

1-5 VDC SIGNALS

$$\left(\frac{\text{FLOW RATE}}{\text{MAX. FLOW}}\right)^2 \times 4 + 1 = \begin{array}{l}\text{OUTPUT SIGNAL}\\\text{(1-5 VDC)}\end{array}$$

$$\sqrt{\frac{\text{OUTPUT SIGNAL} - 1}{4}} \times \begin{array}{l}\text{MAX}\\\text{FLOW}\end{array} = \begin{array}{l}\text{FLOW}\\\text{RATE}\end{array}$$

% DIFF. PRESSURE

$$\left(\frac{\text{FLOW RATE}}{\text{MAX. FLOW}}\right)^2 \left(\begin{smallmatrix}\text{MAX. INCHES}\\\text{OF WATER}\end{smallmatrix}\right) = \begin{smallmatrix}\text{INCHES OF WATER}\\\text{AT THAT FLOW RATE}\end{smallmatrix}$$

$$\sqrt{\frac{\text{IN. H2O AT FLOW RATE}}{\text{MAX. INCHES H2O}}} \times \begin{smallmatrix}\text{MAX}\\\text{FLOW}\end{smallmatrix} = \begin{smallmatrix}\text{FLOW}\\\text{RATE}\end{smallmatrix}$$

3-15 PSIG SQ. ROOT FLOW EXAMPLE:
FLOW RANGE = 0-40 GPM
WHAT WOULD THE OUTPUT BE IF THE
FLOW IS 20 GPM?
ANSWER = 6 PSIG

$$\left(\frac{20 \text{ GPM}}{40 \text{ GPM}}\right)^2 \times 12 + 3 = \begin{smallmatrix}\text{OUTPUT SIGNAL}\\\text{IS 6 PSIG}\end{smallmatrix}$$

BALL PARK ORIFICE RANGE FORMULA

- ONLY WHEN USING THE SAME ORIFICE AND ALL
  OPERATING CONDITIONS ARE THE SAME.

$$\begin{smallmatrix}\text{NEW}\\\text{TRANS.}\\\text{RANGE}\end{smallmatrix} = \left(\begin{smallmatrix}\text{OLD}\\\text{TRANS.}\\\text{RANGE}\end{smallmatrix}\right)\left(\frac{\text{NEW FLOW}}{\text{OLD FLOW}}\right)^2$$

- TYPICALLY KEEP "H2O BETWEEN 20 & 250

$$\begin{smallmatrix}\text{NEW}\\\text{FLOW}\end{smallmatrix} = \left(\begin{smallmatrix}\text{OLD}\\\text{FLOW}\end{smallmatrix}\right)\sqrt{\frac{\text{NEW TRANS. RANGE}}{\text{OLD TRANS. RANGE}}}$$

UPSTREAM & DOWNSTREAM

The exact upstream and downstream pipe diameters of unobstructed pipe that is needed for an orifice run depends upon the beta ratio. In most cases you will need at least 15 upstream and 5 downstream to ensure accuracy.

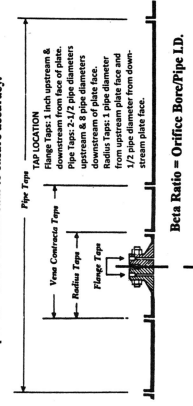

TAP LOCATION

Flange Taps: 1 inch upstream & downstream from face of plate.

Pipe Taps: 2-1/2 pipe diameters upstream & 8 pipe diameters downstream of plate face.

Radius Taps: 1 pipe diameter from upstream plate face and 1/2 pipe diameter from downstream plate face.

Pipe Taps

Vena Contracta Taps

Radius Taps

Flange Taps

Beta Ratio = Orifice Bore/Pipe I.D.

IMPULSE TAP LOCATIONS FOR VERTICAL ORIFICE FLOWMETERS
STEAM

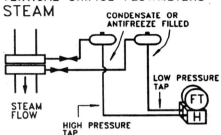

CONDENSATE OR ANTIFREEZE FILLED

STEAM FLOW

LOW PRESSURE TAP

HIGH PRESSURE TAP

IMPULSE TAP LOCATIONS FOR VERTICAL ORIFICE FLOWMETERS WET GAS OR VAPOR

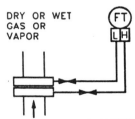

DRY OR WET GAS OR VAPOR

* NOTE ALL TRANSMITTERS HAVE 3-VALVE INSTRUMENT MANIFOLDS.

IMPULSE TAP LOCATIONS FOR HORIZONTAL ORIFICE FLOWMETERS
LIQUIDS

FILLING TEE

BUBBLES CAN GIVE FALSE READINGS HERE.

SEDIMENT CAN FALL INTO THE TRANSMITTER HERE.

SEAL FLUID

* SIDE IMPULSE TAPS ARE BEST

IMPULSE TAP LOCATIONS FOR HORIZONTAL ORIFICE FLOWMETERS
STEAM

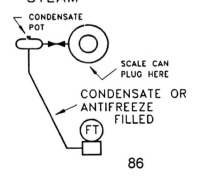

CONDENSATE POT

SCALE CAN PLUG HERE

CONDENSATE OR ANTIFREEZE FILLED

IMPULSE TAP LOCATIONS FOR HORIZONTAL ORIFICE FLOWMETERS
GAS OR VAPORS

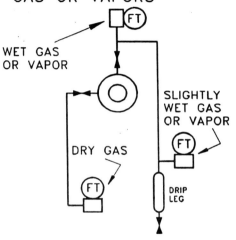

WET GAS OR VAPOR

SLIGHTLY WET GAS OR VAPOR

DRY GAS

DRIP LEG

* NOTE ALL TRANSMITTERS HAVE 3-VALVE INSTRUMENT MANIFOLDS.

SCALE FACTORS (linear)

Usually rotameters in manufacturer's catalogs are based upon either water flow or air flow at standard conditions. Their scales will be either in percent of flow or actual engineering units (SCFH, GPM, etc.). If you use a different fluid, such as hexene, you must first calculate the full range flow of hexene, then a meter factor. It is best to use the formula provided in the catalog to find the full range flow.

EXAMPLE: The selected rotameter has a 0-100% scale and the catalog shows 0-100 GPH of water. The catalog's formula tells us that if we use hexene, the full scale flow will be 117 GPH. To determine the flow factor, divide the maximum hexene flow by the maximum scale value. The answer is 1.17.

$$\text{SCALE FLOW FACTOR} = \frac{117 \text{ GPH}}{100 \%}$$

Therefore, the flow factor is 1.17 times the reading. If the float indicated 41%, the hexene flow would be about 48%.

SCALE FACTORS
(For orifice flowmeter with square root scale)

$$\text{FLOW FACTOR} = \frac{\text{MAX FLOW (GPM, SCFM, etc.)}}{\text{MAX SQ. ROOT SCALE VALUE}}$$

EXAMPLE: Max flow is 7 GPM and the scales is 0-30. Therefore multiply the scale reading by .2334 (flow factor) to obtain the actual flow rate. A scale reading of 18.3 is a flow of 4.271 GPM.

(For orifice flowmeters using a linear scale)
* Not recommended because it is too complex.

$$\text{FLOW FACTOR} = \sqrt{\frac{\text{SCALE READING}}{\text{MAX SCALE}}} \times \text{MAX FLOW RATE}$$

EXAMPLE: Max flow is 20 SCFH. The scale reading is 6.8 on a 0-15 linear scale. Take the square root of 6.8 divided by 15 which is .6733 then multiply .6733 (flow factor) by 20 SCFH to get a flow rate of 13.466 SCFH.

LINEAR TRANSMITTER FORMULAS

3-15 PSIG SIGNALS, LEVEL

$$\left(\frac{\% \text{ LEVEL}}{100}\right) \times 12 + 3 = \text{OUTPUT SIGNAL} \ (3-15 \text{ PSIG})$$

$$\frac{\text{OUTPUT SIGNAL} - 3}{12} \times 100 = \% \text{ LEVEL}$$

4-20 MA SIGNALS, LEVEL

$$\left(\frac{\% \text{ LEVEL}}{100}\right) \times 16 + 4 = \text{OUTPUT SIGNAL} \ (4-20 \text{ MA})$$

$$\frac{\text{OUTPUT SIGNAL} - 4}{16} \times 100 = \% \text{ LEVEL}$$

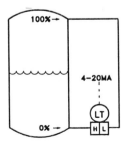

Level Example: What is the 4-20ma output signal of the transmitter when the level glass indicates 48% level? Divide 100 into 48, then multiply it by 16 & add 4. The answer is 11.68 mA, which represents a 48% level output signal. If using a pneumatic transmitter, the answer would be 8.76 psig.

UNIVERSAL LINEAR FORMULA

TRANSMITTER INPUT   TRANSMITTER OUTPUT

$$\frac{\left(\begin{array}{c}\text{INPUT}\\\text{VALUE}\end{array}\right) - \left(\begin{array}{c}\text{START OF}\\\text{RANGE}\end{array}\right)}{\text{INPUT SPAN}} = \frac{\left(\begin{array}{c}\text{OUTPUT}\\\text{VALUE}\end{array}\right) - \left(\begin{array}{c}\text{START OF}\\\text{RANGE}\end{array}\right)}{\text{OUTPUT SPAN}}$$

TEMPERATURE EXAMPLE:
RTD TRANS. RANGE = 20 TO 100 DEG. F
TRANS. SIGNAL = 4-20 MA
WHAT IS THE INPUT TEMP. FOR A TRANS. OUTPUT
OF 14.28 MA?
ANSWER = 71.4 DEG. F

$$\frac{X - 20}{80} = \frac{14.28 - 4}{16}$$

X - 20 = 51.4   THEREFORE X = 71.4 DEG. F

Maintenance Tip
When a control valve is used as part of a split-range loop or if the action of a valve is reversed by using the valve positioner, do not bypass it.

Leaking Checking Pneumatic Tubing With A Bubbler

A good method to check for leaks in pneumatic instrument tubing or transmission lines is by using a bubbler. The tubing to be tested should be capped off at one end and pressured up to about 15 psig from the other end. Any leakage is registered by the amount of makeup seen as bubbles in the bubbler. The bubbler is more sensitive than a rotameter. The dip tube in in the bubbler should be immersed one inch into the water.

1) Close valves 1, 2, & 3. Set the pressure gauge to 15 psig by adjusting the regulator. Receiver bellows and other devices, if left connected to the tubing could be damaged by pressures above 15 psig.
2) Connect the bubbler to the tubing to be tested. Cap off the other end.
3) Open valve 1 and allow time for the entire system to equalize. It may take up to 5 minutes for very long runs. The pressure gauge should be showing a constant pressure once it equalizes. Then pressure gauge should be showing a constant pressure once it equalizes, providing that you do not have a big leak.
4) Open valve 2 then block valve 1. Slowly open valve 3. If the tubing has a leak, bubbles will be seen in the bubbler. Use a soap and water solution to find leaks. Don't allow leaks of more than 5 bubbles per minute.
5) With no more leaks to resolve, close valve 2 & 3 and depressure the system.

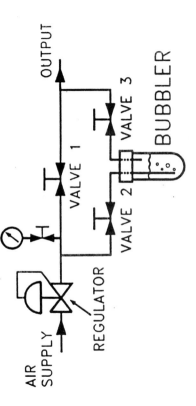

AIR SUPPLY

REGULATOR

VALVE 1

VALVE 2

VALVE 3

OUTPUT

BUBBLER

90 DEGREE V-NOTCH WEIR

FORMULA FOR GPM OF WATER FLOWING OVER A 90 Degree V-NOTCH WEIR.

$$1140 \left(\frac{INCHES}{12}\right)^{2.475} = GPM$$

6" HEIGHT = 205.048 GPM

6 INCHES

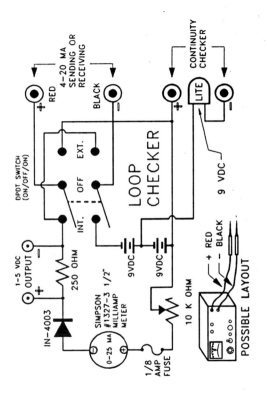

4-20 MA SENDING OR RECEIVING

RED +

BLACK −

CONTINUITY CHECKER

LITE

LOOP CHECKER

9 VDC

DPDT SWITCH (ON/OFF/ON)

EXT.

OFF

INT.

9VDC 9VDC

1-5 VDC OUTPUT −

+

250 OHM

SIMPSON #1327-3 1/2" MILIAMP METER

10 K OHM

IN-4003

0-25 MA

1/8 AMP FUSE

+ RED
− BLACK

POSSIBLE LAYOUT

Loop Checker Here is a device for loop check outs in non classified areas but not for accurate calibrations. It has several features. It can simulate a field transmitter, drive a 4-20mA signal into an I/P transducer for stroking a control valve, for checking relay contact continuity or to produce a 1-5 VDC input signal for recorders.

Simulator The red and black test jacks are normally hooked to a field transmitter, The DPDT switch has three positions: **INT**ernally powered, **OFF** and **EXT**ernally powered. If the transmitter is loop powered from the controller or DCS, the switch should be in EXT. Simulation is done by adjusting the 10K ohm potentiometer for any value from 4 to 20 mA on the meter.

Valve Stroker With the switch in the INT. position and the red and black test jacks hooked to an I/P, you can stroke a control valve by turning the 10K ohm pot to the 4-20 mA value needed.

Voltage Generator With the switch in INT. position and the red and black test jacks shorted together, you can produce a 1-5 VDC output signal. The voltage will appear across the 250 ohm resistor. Since the meter is in mA, you will have to translate the value to 1-5 VDC or use a DVOM to view the voltage directly.

Continuity Checker With the switch in any position you can test for continuity by connecting across the two continuity test jacks. The 9 VDC light will be on if you have continuity across contacts, in the circuit or a questionable bulb under test.

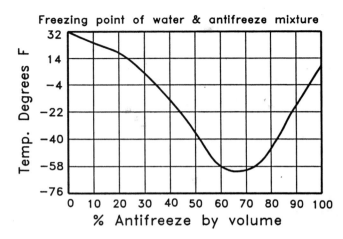

Freezing point of water & antifreeze mixture

Temp. Degrees F (y-axis): 32, 14, −4, −22, −40, −58, −76

% Antifreeze by volume (x-axis): 0, 10, 20, 30, 40, 50, 60, 70, 80, 90, 100

Notice that the optimum mixture is about 65% antifreeze and 35% water. A 50/50 mixture of water and antifreeze protects instruments from freezing down to about -34 degrees F.

Using an antifreeze which has a color helps to show its presence.

==================================

Maintenance Tip

A common mistake is to install control valves and pressure reducing regulators backwards.

Troubleshooting Tips

Visual Checks: Look for obvious problems; broken wires, moisture, corrosion, plugged impulse taps, charred circuit board, wires crossed or parts installed wrong.

Substitution: Some problems can easily be found by replacing or substituting parts, circuit board or components.

Simulation: If you can accurately simulate field conditions on the bench, instrument and control problems may be solved. But be sure that type of input signal or process conditions are the same as in the field.

Divide & Conquer: When you have a loss of voltage or a signal, find a mid-point (divide the signal path) and test for it. Depending upon whether you find the signal or not, either divide it upstream or downstream and test again.

Elimination: Some instrument problems could be from the process, the installation, the electronics, some type of interference or equipment failure. Try to use methods, such as simulation or substitution, that can prove each part is not the problem. This is a method to eliminate each area so that the true problem will be revealed.

Consultation: Many difficult problems can easily be fixed if you ask the right person for advice. Often you can find experienced operators, engineer or maintenance people who have encountered the same problem before. Use their experience to give you a direction to investigate.

Install Helps: Troubleshooting can be made a lot easier if you install gauges, meters, relays with indication neon bulbs, recorders or other devices that tell you what the instrument or process is doing.

Fresh Start: After fighting a difficult problem for a long time, step back and look at it with new eyes. Think of all of the things that could cause those symptoms. Check all of it again as if it were a new problem. Don't assume anything is correct, even your test equipment.

Other Tips: Intermittent electronic problems that are heat related may be found using a hot air gun to warm the circuit board. Use care not to overheat the components. Problems with duplicate addresses may be resolved by deleting each device until communication with the computer is restored.

Shotgun Method: One of the fastest yet costly ways to find a problem is to replace every circuit card, relay or plug-in device in the entire instrument.

It may get the equipment working quickly, but you seldom have a clue as to which part was the offending component.

375 Emerson/Rosemount HART communicator connections

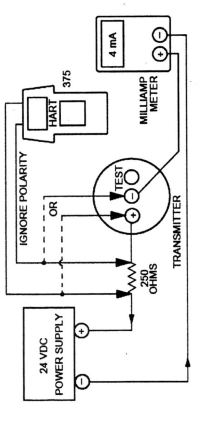

Solenoid & Relay Power Consumption

The power consumption may be determined from the catalog information. Usually the maximum current will be about 80% of the fuse size. See the AC formulas below.

$$\text{AMPS (INRUSH)} = \frac{\text{volt-amp ``inrush''}}{\text{voltage}}$$

$$\text{AMPS (HOLDING)} = \frac{\text{volt-amp ``holding''}}{\text{voltage}}$$

For DC relays and solenoids use:

$$\text{AMPS} = \frac{\text{watts (DC)}}{\text{voltage}}$$

CHECK OUT FUNDAMENTALS When new instrumentation is installed, several checks should be made. Among them are; wire checks, function checks, failsafe actions and logic checks.

1) Wire Checks: The wiring should be checked for secure and correct connections, proper wire size, proper labeling, continuity, shorting to ground and excessive resistance (Typically, short wire runs will have less than 4Ω, long runs will have less than 12Ω). These checks should be done without the loop fuses installed. High Voltage cables are tested for faults by using a DC Hypot (Thumper) tester.

2) Function Checks: (For Analog Inputs) After the transmitters have been bench calibrated and tagged, install them in the field. Install loop fuses. Use actual process changes (first choice) or loop simulators (like the Altek) and test to see if the DCS receives the signal at 0%, 50% and 100% (in both directions, increasing and decreasing). For analog outputs to control valves, stroke the control valve from the DCS and see if it responds at 0%, 50% and 100% (in both directions, increasing and decreasing).

3) Failsafe Checks: In addition to the function test that manipulates (or is simulated) the process to an alarm condition, a check should be made if a wire breaks.

* (For control valves) In turn, remove the 4-20 ma signal to the transducer, the air supply and the 3-15 psig air signal to the control valve or positioner to check for proper valve failure.

* Simple process-powered pressure (or level, temperature, flow, etc.) switches should have a contact wire lifted to determine how it fails.

* Speed and temperature switches with electronics have two failsafe action possibilities, the failure of the power and the failure or the opening of the contacts or wiring. First test for power failsafe action, by removing the power and see the results. Restore the power. Next, test the contacts by lifting a wire of the contacts and see the results.

4) Logic Checks: For Large interlock systems, test and simulate the logic and schematics beforehand by using another DCS system. For smaller or less complicated interlocks, force points or jumper them to verify their proper action.

POSSIBLE SOLUTIONS TO LEVEL PROBLEMS

SEAL LEG OPTIONS:
1. VAPOR LOOP
2. SEAL FLUID
3. VAPOR CONDENSOR
4. STEAM TRACING
5. DRIP LEG
6. AUTO. LIQUID TRAP
7. CONTINOUS SEAL
   LEG FLUSH
8. 1:1 PNEU. BOOSTER
9. REMOTE DIAPHRAGM
   SEAL TRANSMITTER
10. MOORE PRODUCTS
    19K1 BUBBLER
11. AIR, N2 OR WATER
    FLUSH TO KEEP TAPS
    CLEAR OF SOLIDS.
    (USE A PURGE RELAY)

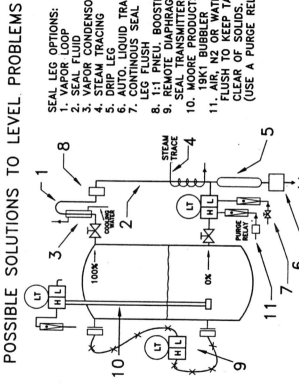

Tank Blanketing Regulator

Too often the nitrogen tank blanketing regulators are not installed properly. It is best to have the downstream sensing line separate from the regulator discharge line. If the sensing line feels any back pressure, it will oscillate. That is why full bore block valves and tubing or pipe that is large enough should be used. With back pressure, the regulator's constant opening and closing will wear out its valve trim and/or diaphragm. The sensing line must sense the tank pressure instead of the regulator's output. See the drawing below for a **proper** installation.

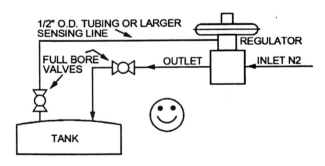

In the drawing below, notice the **POOR** installation. The sensing line is primarily sensing the regulator's output, instead of the actual tank pressure. The sensing line should have its own connection to the tank without any restrictions.

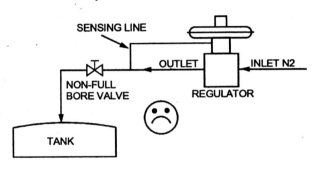

+++++++++++++++++++++++++++++++++++++++

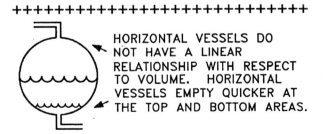

HORIZONTAL VESSELS DO NOT HAVE A LINEAR RELATIONSHIP WITH RESPECT TO VOLUME. HORIZONTAL VESSELS EMPTY QUICKER AT THE TOP AND BOTTOM AREAS.

Fill Up and Drain Out Level Control

The solenoid operated valve (SOV) is an energize to open (N.C.) solenoid valve. Both S1 and S2 are mounted to hang down in the Normally Closed position. When fully lifted their contacts will open. Both float switches have about 6" of float movement hysteresis. R1 is a latching relay with its N.O. contacts across S1. The tank level drains according to the demands of the process. This level control system will automatically fill the tank as needed using an on/off action. When the tank is empty the SOV will be open so the water will fill the tank. When the water makes S1 float, S1 opens but R1 remains latched in. When the tank level makes S2 float, S1 and S2 will be open, R1 unlatches and the SOV is de-energized. Therefore the tank stops filling. As the water drains out, the S2 float drops to its closed position, S1 is still open, the SOV remains de-energized and R1 in unlatched.

When the tank level drains down to the non-floating position of S1, both S1 and S2 will be closed, the SOV will energize and R1 latches. Therefore the water starts filling the tank.

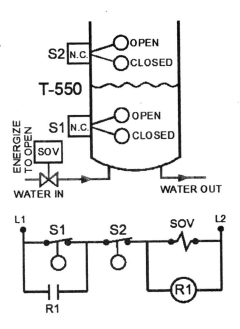

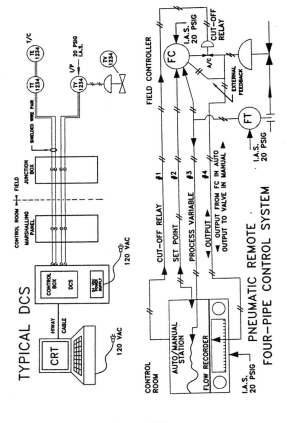

TYPICAL DCS

PNEUMATIC REMOTE
FOUR-PIPE CONTROL SYSTEM

108

Tech Tip: Use this short extension cord test rig to easily measure the current in a power cord.

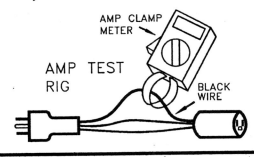

Constant Differential Flow Controller Purge
Notice the drawing of the constant differential flow controller. Notice that it keeps a constant 3 psi difference between the process pressure and the regulator pressure because of the 3 lb bias spring pressure on top of the diaphragm. As the process changes, the regulator adjusts and always keeps the difference at 3 psi. That situation will allow the rotameter flow to be steady and therefore allow for the transmitter to accurately measure the process pressure.

PURGE FOR A PRESSURE TAP

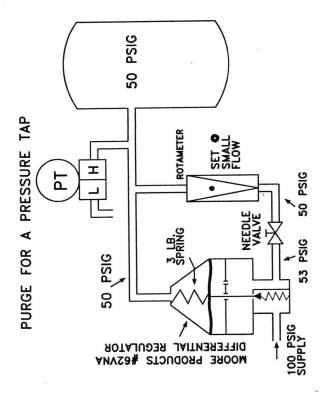

RATIO CONTROLS

Ratio control loops consist of two flows: the wild flow and the captive flow. The wild flow is the one that is not being controlled. It can increase or decrease as needed by the process conditions. The other flow is the captive flow. It is the one that will be controlled at a ratio of the wild flow. Often ratio loops are used for blending two fluid streams and they need to be at a specific flow to keep the correct mix ratio.

The simplest ratio control scheme is where the wild flow transmitter's output is being used as the setpoint for the captive flow controller. It is a fixed ratio system based upon the flowmeter ranges. However, their flow transmitters can be re-ranged so that it will be fixed for a new ratio. The most common ratio scheme uses a FFC (flow to flow controller) which allows the operator to dial in his desired ratio. That way the captive flow will then be controlled any ratio that the process needs. It has a lot more flexibility than the simple ratio loop.

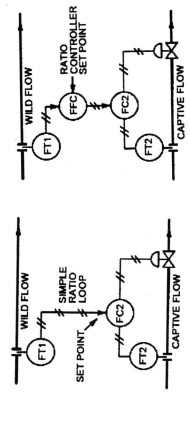

A fixed ratio control loop.   An adjustable ratio control loop.

112